By Stephen G. Bowling

SIMON

HERBERT

Simon's Rocket to the Moon

LILLY

CLARENCE

Illustrated by Vitali Dudarenka

Simon's Tree House Adventures Series
Simon's Tree Party
Simon's Search for the Scary Dragon
Simon's Rocket to the Moon

Also by Stephen G. Bowling
and Vitali Dudarenka

Calvin the Christmas Tree

www.StephenGBowling.com

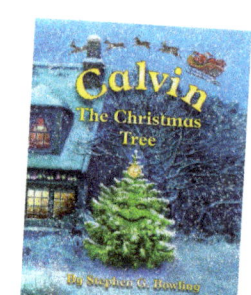

Publisher's Cataloging-in-Publication Data

Names: Bowling, Stephen G., 1960- author. | Dudarenka, Vitali, 1965- illustrator.
Title: Simon's rocket to the moon / Stephen G. Bowling ; Vitali Dudarenka, illustrator.
Description: Stamford, CT : Valley of Mexico, 2022. | Series: Simon's tree house adventures, bk. 3. | Summary: A young bird and his barnyard friends decide to build a rocket to visit the Moon. | Audience: Grades K-3.
Identifiers: LCCN 2022900687 (print) | ISBN 978-1-950957-20-0 (paperback) | ISBN 978-1-950957-21-7 (hardcover) | ISBN 978-1-950957-22-4 (ebook : epub) | ISBN 978-1-950957-23-1 (ebook : Kindle)
Subjects: LCSH: Picture books for children. | High interest-low vocabulary books. | CYAC: Birds--Fiction. | Farm life--Fiction. | Friendship--Fiction. | Moon--Fiction. | BISAC: JUVENILE FICTION / Animals / Birds. | JUVENILE FICTION / Animals / Farm Animals. | JUVENILE FICTION / Readers / Beginner.
Classification: LCC PZ7.1.B69 Si 2022 (print) | LCC PZ7.1.B69 (ebook) | DDC [E]--dc23.

Copyright © 2022 Stephen G. Bowling

All rights reserved. No part of this publication may be reproduced, distributed, or transmitted in any form or by any means, including photocopying, recording, or other electronic or mechanical methods, without the prior written permission of the publisher, except in the case of brief quotations embodied in critical reviews and certain other noncommercial uses permitted by copyright law. For permission requests, contact the publisher below.

Valley of Mexico, Inc., Stamford, CT
info@valleyofmexico.com

On a clear summer night,
    halfway into June,
        Simon lay in bed
            looking at the moon.

"Who lives there," he thought,
    "on that place far away?
        What songs do they sing?
            What games do they play?"

"Do they eat ice cream?
    Do they drink milkshakes?
        When they have birthday parties
            do they serve special cakes?"

The next day he told his friends
what he planned to do.

"I'm going to the Moon," he said,
"and you can all come too.

Let's build a big rocket ship
that soars through the air.

We can fly it to the Moon
and make new friends up there."

"Then we'll try their chocolate pudding
and the cookies that they bake.

We can try all the candy,
while we taste every cake."

"What a great idea." said Lilly,
"Let's start right away.

If we work really fast,
we can go there today."

Clarence drew a picture
of the rocket they would make,

that showed how to build it
and the time it should take.

He checked all the details.
He even checked them twice.

He went to the Owl
to ask for his advice.

"You need many things," said Owl,
"to build a rocket ship,

and you must decide
what to take on your trip."

Then a mighty search began
 to see what they could find,

  to build the spaceship
   that Clarence had designed.

Simon found some metal
 and gathered lots of wood.

  He looked for some cardboard
   and found all he could.

Lilly searched through the barn
and found empty cans.

Then she flew around once more
and found rubber bands.

Herbert found three boxes,
two pots and a pan.

"These will work well," he thought,
"according to the plan."

Four very long screws
and a big box of nails

were found with some string
beside two garden pails.

Clarence brought some glue
plus a large roll of tape.

He knew these could help
to get the rocket in shape.

Everything they found
was paced in a pile.

Building their great ship
might take them a while.

They pieced things together
and secured all the parts,

following the instructions
Clarence wrote on his charts.

They hammered and they sawed.
They nailed and they screwed.

They tied and they wired.
They taped and they glued.

The ship was painted red,
  with parts painted white.

These colors should look nice
  when the rocket takes flight.

A basket full of snacks
  was prepared for the trip.

And quite a few toys
  were stored in the ship.

The craft stood tall
   as it pointed to the sky.

      It was aimed at the Moon
         and soon it would fly.

But the sun was going down.
   It was starting to get late.

      Dinner time was soon
         so the trip will have to wait.

They went straight home
   to eat with their parents,

      and told of the mission
         and designs made by Clarence.

Every detail was explained
   of the spaceship they created,

      all the plans that were made,
         and the trip that awaited.

When this long day was over,
   they were tucked in their beds,

      with thoughts of new adventures
         still swirling in their heads.

They drifted off to sleep
   remembering the day,

      planning how the rocket
         would finally make its way.

The ship will surely fly,
   and travel so it seems.

      It will all go as planned
         if only in their dreams.

Simon's Fun Facts about the Moon

The Moon is 4,500,000,000 years old! (4.5 Billion)

The Moon circles the Earth really fast. It travels at 2,282 Miles per Hour. (3,673 Km/hr)

The Moon doesn't produce its own light. We see the Moon because it reflects light from the Sun.

It gets super hot and super cold on the Moon - as hot as 260°F (127°C) and as cold as −243°F (-153°C) every day!

If you dropped a rock on the Moon it would fall really slowly. That's because the Moon's gravity (the force that pulls things toward the ground) is much weaker than the Earth's gravity.

The average distance from the Earth to the Moon is 238,857 miles (384,403 kilometers). If you drove a car to the Moon at 65 miles per hour (about 100 kph) it would take you 153 days without ever stopping to eat, to sleep, or to use the bathroom.

If you were on the Moon, the sky would look black because there is no atmosphere.

www.StephenGBowling.com

Simon's Tree House Adventures Series

Simon's Tree Party

Simon's Search for the Scary Dragon

Simon's Rocket to the Moon

 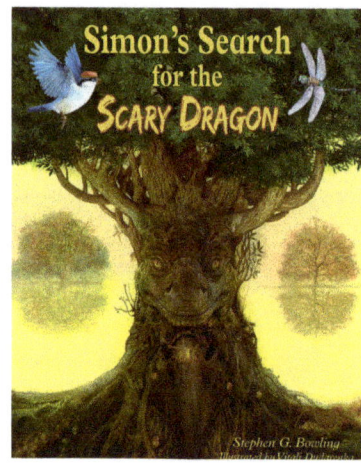 

Also by
Stephen G. Bowling
and Vitali Dudarenka

*Calvin
the Christmas Tree*

Sign up for our email list and get news, previews, free stuff and more.

www.StephenGBowling.com